Animals Everywhere

ILLUSTRATED BY ASANTOSG

STORY BY MARI SUMALEE

Africa

Hyena

Impala

Ostrich

Wildebeest

Africa

Gorilla

Camel

Cheetah

Hippopotamus

Africa

Monkey

Vulture

Oryx-Gazelle

Crocodile

Africa

Giraffe

Flamingo

Lion

Zebra

Africa

Meerkat

Rinosarus

Chimpanzee

Elephant

Arctic

Emperor
Penguin

Polar Bear

Puffin

Walrus

Arctic

Gray Wolf

Seal

Reindeer

Albatross

Arctic

Penguin

Killer Whale

Puffin

Snow Owl

Antarctica

Penguins

Seals

Walrus

Asia

Panda

Monkey

Tiger

Elephant

Asia

Horse

Reindeer

Quail

Wildcat

Australia

Crocodile

Koala

Seagulls

Kangaroos

Australia

Europe

Owl

Squirrel

Badger

Porcupine

Europe

Fox

Moose

Quail

Magpie

Forest

Frog

Eagle

Chameleon

Hedgehog

Forest

Owl

Wolf

Raccoon

Bear

Forest

Beaver

Spider

Otter

Snail

Fairly tale

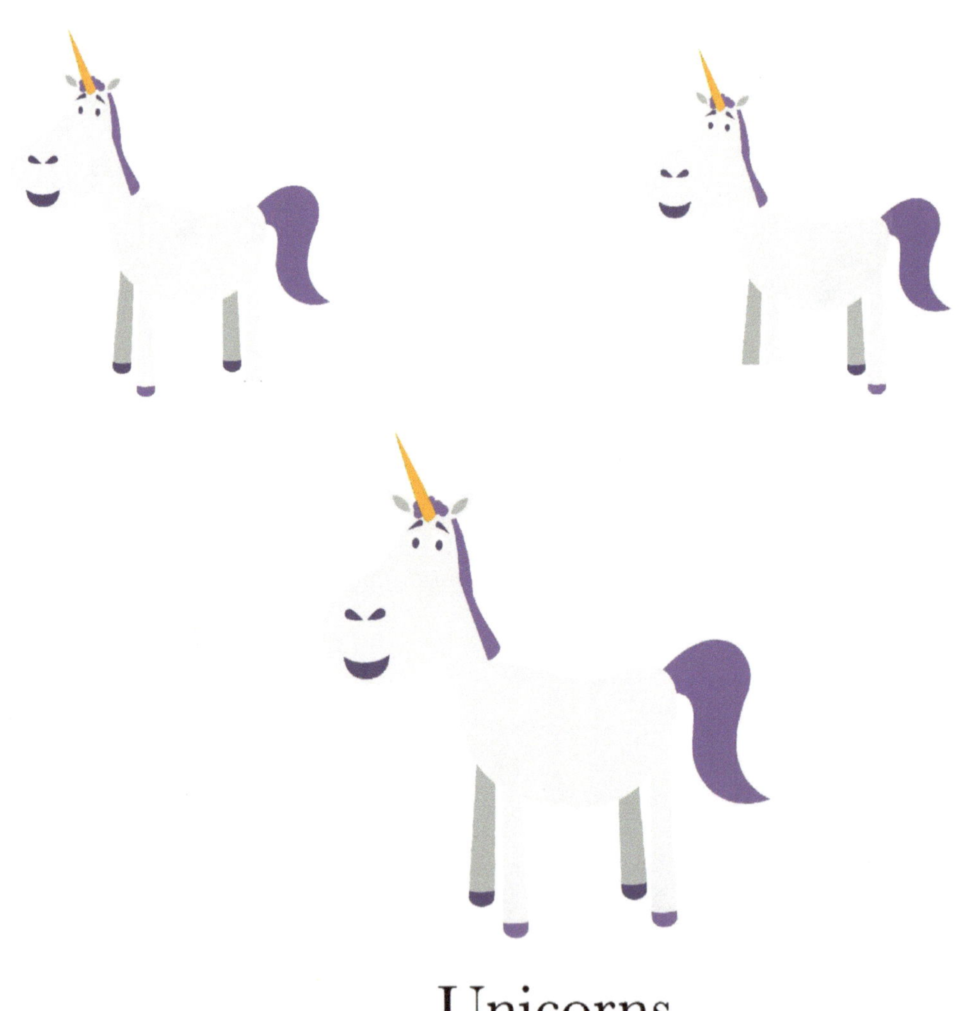

Unicorns

Jungle

Buffalo

Rabbit

Lemur

Badger

Jungle

Quail

Frog

Bat

Parrot

Jungle

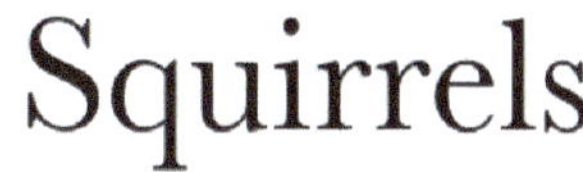

Exotic birds

Squirrels

Northern Asia

New Zealand

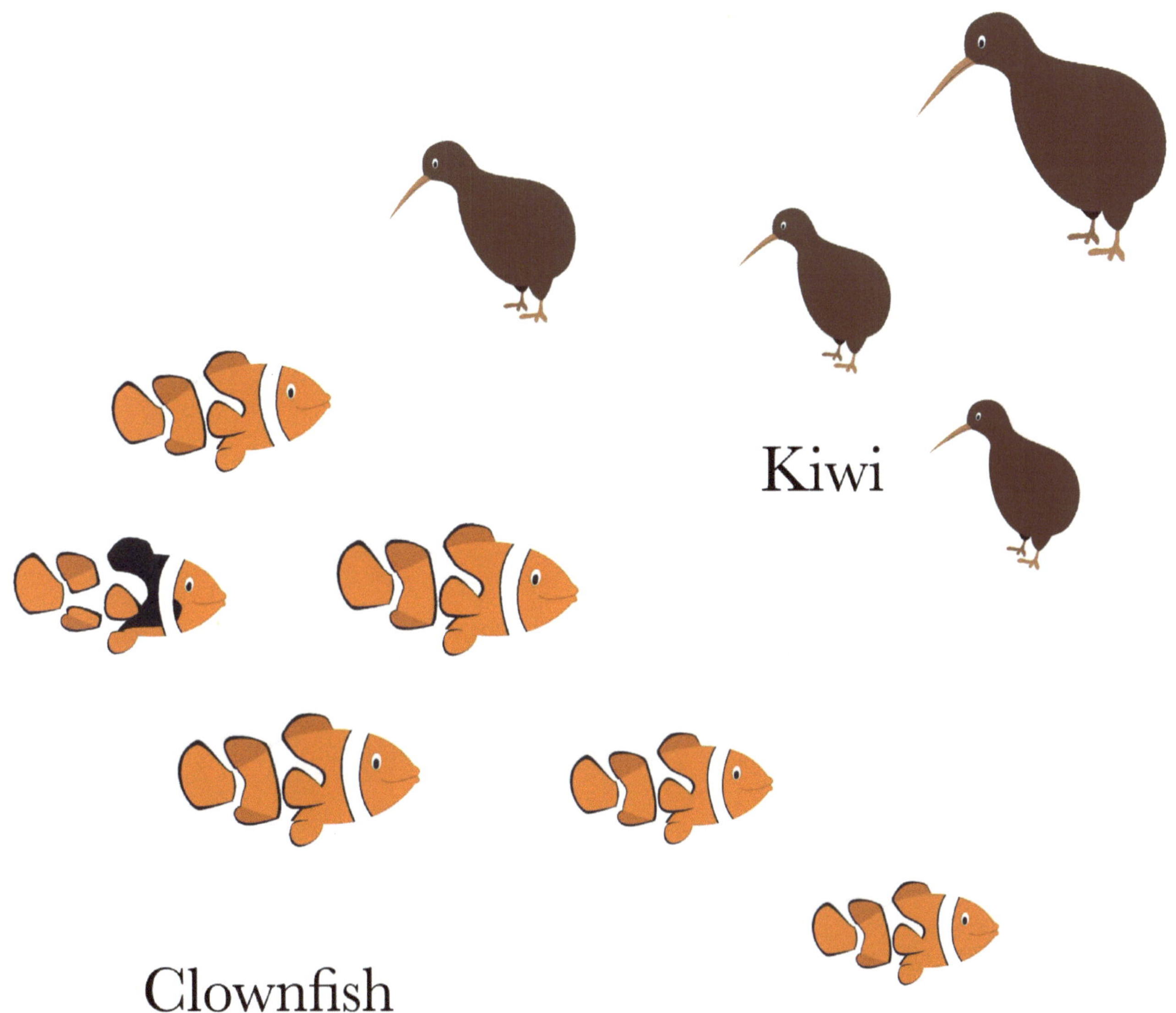

Ocean

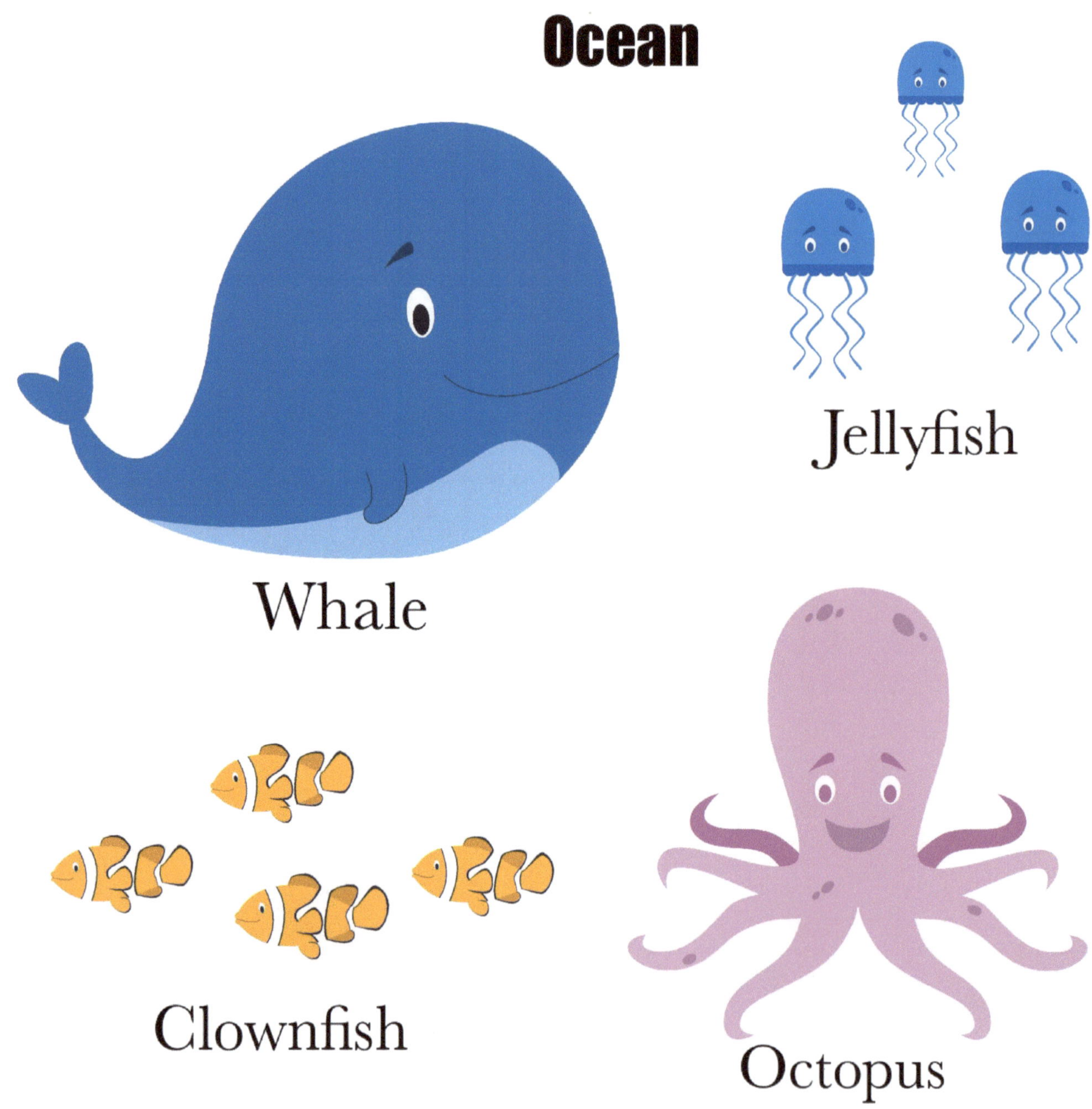

Ocean

Dolphins

Ocean

South America

Llama

Turtle

Alligator

Frog

South America

Sloth

Amazon Toucan

Python

Parrot